LETTERS TO MY DAUGHTER

Randal,

Always remember

you are

badass !

Elisa

LETTERS TO MY DAUGHTER

HOW TO STEP OUT OF OTHER PEOPLE'S BOXES AND INTO YOUR LIFE AS A CONFIDENT, WHOLEHEARTED, BADASS QUEEN.

ELISA M. HAYS

This is a work of nonfiction. The events and conversations in this book have been set down to the best of the author's ability. Some parts have been fictionalized in various degrees, for various reasons.

For more information, address: elisa@elisahays.com

SECOND EDITION

Published by Connecting Dots, LLC

www.ElisaHays.com

Dedicated with love to badass daughters everywhere.

ACKNOWLEDGMENTS

Without my first mentor, my mother, I could never have become the resilient woman I am today. She taught me from an early age to question assumptions and never limit how far I could go. She defied expectations and pushed her personal boundaries. Through the way she lives her life, she demonstrates how to fully own her feminine power, without ever making it anti-men. I've never doubted my mother is a superhero.

No acknowledgments I write could be complete without mentioning my family. They deserve more praise, credit, and gratitude than I can possibly express. Thank you to Steve, Claire, Alex, and Sarah for putting up with my craziness and always supporting my wild ideas. You are my whole world.

"You know, you do need mentors, but in the end, you really just need to believe in yourself."
DIANA ROSS

CONTENTS

INTRODUCTION

This collection of "letters" comes directly out of my extraor-dinarily personal, often painful, experiences. Though I spent fifteen years mentoring young women in my company, that isn't why I wrote this book. I wrote it because, sometimes, you can only learn what really matters when life hits you like a big rig truck. When life knocks you down, you under-stand the importance of knowing how to step out of other people's boxes and into your life as a confident, whole-hearted, badass queen.

On March 1, 2014, everything went sideways. Two employees and I were driving from Washington state to the Houston Livestock Show and Rodeo in Texas to perform a children's show I owned called, *The Cutest Show on Earth*. We traveled in a Ford F-250 pickup truck, named Fiona, pulling a sixteen-foot cargo trailer. In Oklahoma, an hour south of Wichita, we suddenly found ourselves caught in an epic ice storm. The trailer slid sideways, out of control. We became stuck, jackknifed on a two-lane highway. Sitting in the driver seat, I was the only one who saw what was coming in the rear-view mirror—the headlights of an eighteen-wheeler semi-truck. We would be hit in just a few seconds.

What I didn't know, was that what was coming at us was a semi-truck, followed by a Toyota Sequoia SUV, followed by another semi-truck. Moments before they careened into us, I rapidly evacuated the two twenty-one-year-old women from our truck. Thankfully, they arrived safely to the side of the road without serious injuries. Unfortunately, as I was the last to run for safety, I did not fare as well. I was hit by a semi-truck going sixty-five miles per hour...and I wasn't in a vehicle. The driver, with the truck on cruise-control, never touched the brakes. His vehicle launched my body into the air before he drove over our F-250 and drug it down the highway until finally coming to a stop.

Emergency Medical Technicians found my body ninety feet away, impaled on a cable guardrail in the center median of the highway, bleeding to death. I suffered a traumatic brain injury, broken left wrist, broken left leg, broken ribs, a collapsed lung, punctured diaphragm, lacerated left kidney, and that wasn't the bad news. My shattered pelvis had essentially folded in half and my tailbone was pulverized.

The storm made airlift impossible. Emergency crews rushed me sixty-five miles in an ambulance to the nearest Level-1 trauma hospital in Wichita, Kansas.

They raced my body through the doors of the Emergency Department with my eyes fixed and dilated, with no pulse, and with me unable to breathe on my own. Blood poured out of my ripped-open left side. Over 1,800 miles away, my family learned the shocking news that my chance of surviving the night was miniscule.

My husband Steve and I have three children. Our oldest, Claire, was a junior in high school. Alex, our middle child, was in the ninth grade. And our youngest, Sarah, was in the eighth grade. At thirteen years old, after hearing the news, she retreated to her bedroom in shock. She sat on her bed, scrolling through photos of me on her phone, trying to imagine how she would bury her mother. But I made it through that first night. And the next night. And the next.

Halfway through my seven-week stay in the surgical intensive care unit, just as doctors believed they had gotten me through the worst of it, I developed sepsis and nearly died again. They raced me into emergency surgery, this time to remove all of my gluteal muscles on the left side where the infection raged, poisoning my bloodstream. That horrific and rare surgery was one of more than twenty major surgeries I would go through over the course of my fight to stay alive. Saving my life required seven hospitals in four states spanning the North American continent, including a high-risk kidney transplant with my younger brother as the donor.

It has been a hell of a ride, to say the least. Astoundingly though, I wouldn't trade what I've learned for anything. As of this writing, I'm working on writing a full account of the dramatic, at times surprisingly comical, saga of my survival and personal transformation in memoir titled, *Semi Tragic*. You can download two free chapters and stay informed of the book release date by signing up on my website at https://www.ElisaHays.com/freebies.

Over the years since the accident, I've been blessed to talk with my daughters and many other young women about how to live with strength, empathy, and resilience. What a joy to watch my girls grow into young women! This book represents lessons I would have wanted someone to share with them, had I not survived that horrific night in 2014. *Letters to My Daughter* contains a collection of mentoring topics, tidbits, and tips for women of all ages.

We need more strong women in the world, and it starts with our daughters. This book will help anyone teach the young women in their lives. It's for parents, coaches, teachers, and mentors looking for a way to share practical lessons of personal fortitude and wisdom. It's for anyone lacking a strong female role model—someone who has fought in the trenches. Perhaps, and most importantly, this book is for you. I hope that in these pages you gain the inspiration and motivation to live your very best badass life.

Long may you reign!

—*Elisa Hays*

ONE WOMAN AT A TIME

"I don't think of myself as a feminist. I think of myself as a woman in the world trying to do what I want to do."
Rebecca Sullivan, MD

*W*hen I think of the women who have taught me lessons for success, the first one at the top of the list is my Mom, Rebecca Sullivan. Mom wouldn't consider herself a "wild feminist," but she did do amazing things within male-dominated industries that paved the way for many women to follow. Instead of allowing unfair obstacles to become setbacks because of her gender, Mom simply worked harder to reach her dreams. In a time when it was unusual to educate women just as we do men, Mom pushed for every opportunity.

My mother's biggest advice to daughters everywhere has always been this: keep challenging yourself.

Do the hard thing. There are still industries out there where women are the exception to the rule. Women have a place in those industries, and our voices need to be heard. Push yourself toward your passion and life will always be satisfying. My incredible mother inspires me and will be an inspiration to daughters everywhere. Keep reading and you'll see why.

REBECCA SULLIVAN: I don't call myself a feminist. I don't think in those terms. I just think of myself as a woman in the world trying to do what I want to do. In some ways I have to look to my father, strangely enough. One thing my father believed was that you should educate the girls just like you do the boys. This was in the 1950s when it was downright weird to educate girls.

My father valued education very much, although he himself did not finish college. After his first semester in college, his mother developed breast cancer. He went home to be with her until she died.

When I was growing up, I learned to never be afraid of new things. For example, he taught me welding for a school project. At his suggestion, I made a steam engine—with his help of course. He was actually a clerk in a plumbing company, but he loved to get down in his workshop and just fiddle around. He was smart and could do a lot of things. As a consequence, when I wanted to go to college, it never occurred to me that I wouldn't.

At that time, if women did go to college, it was often just until they got married. In that time period, women went to college to get their "M.R.S. degree," but that never occurred to me. I felt that you should go to college to get an education in something that challenges you. The sciences had always challenged me, so I earned a Bachelor of Science in Chemistry and a minor in Math, but I didn't stop there. I went on to get a master's degree in Cardiovascular Pharmacology. There were, of course, big time lapses in my education because of getting married and traveling. My husband, Al, was in the Air Force so we moved around a great deal.

I intended to earn a PhD and teach in a medical school. At that time in our family life, the Air Force had stationed my husband in Thule, Greenland, for a year. I debated about where I would go educationally. He happened to be friends with another Air Force officer, a physician, who told him that if I wanted to teach in a medical school, I needed to get an MD. I had actually been thinking about it since high school. It sounds a little strange, but the idea of getting an MD felt as if it would be something I could say at the end of my life, "I've helped people." To do that, for me, seemed like the purpose in life.

Even in a time period when the overwhelming majority of authority figures were men, I wasn't driven to buck the system or make a statement. Nor was I driven by a need for success or to impress others. I wanted to make a difference.

I didn't have female role models in my life much at

all. I was raised by my father. My mother was not nearby. I had a grandmother, but no sisters, or other women around to act as a role model. Not having women in what one might call, at that time particularly, the traditional roles of women, I just assumed I could do whatever I wanted. Like welding. When I had the need, I thought, "Welding? Sure, why not? Let's go!"

I earned my master's degree at Creighton University in Omaha, Nebraska. As part of my degree in Cardiovascular Pharmacology, I had taken some of my classes with the medical students. When I decided to attend medical school, it made sense to apply to Creighton. There were two medical schools in Omaha, the other one being the University of Nebraska, but I had prayed about this and decided that if I was not accepted at Creighton, I would not apply to the University of Nebraska.

I made an appointment with the man who was the Chair of the Acceptance Committee for the medical school. Because he also happened to be on the board for which I did my oral exams for my master's degree, I already knew him. I went in to talk to him about going to medical school and his response was, "Well, why do you want to do that?" I thought that was a pretty dumb question. Why does anybody want to go to medical school except to become a doctor?

I just couldn't bring myself to give him a straight answer. I said, "Oh, it will give me something to do in my spare time." I figured that was a better answer than calling him pretty dumb. Fortunately, he didn't say anything back to me except, "I don't approve of women in medicine." And again, I just couldn't take this seriously because it was such a stupid statement. So, I said, "Well, that's OK. I don't approve of men in medicine." I figured we were pretty even here. After that his response was, "Oh, all right, you can be in."

About three months later they came to me with the application paperwork for the medical school because I hadn't actually done any paperwork. I was already in medical school, doing the classes, doing my dissection and everything. They were very apologetic, but they asked if I would please complete it. This was at a time when the average pre-med student was applying to seventeen medical schools. It was a little funny that I ended up filling out the paperwork just to make the record straight.

There were one hundred and six of us in the class and just four women. In 1972, getting women into medical schools was a brand-new endeavor. Previously, virtually all the medical students had been men.

Professors posted the students' grades on the door of whatever department your class was in. I never looked at those grades. I figured if I had passed, I would be continuing on. If I hadn't passed, someone would surely get in touch with me. I found out I was awarded the outstanding pediatric student after my junior year. When I graduated, I was in the top ten percent of medical students nationally.

I entered into the Air Force and had a very successful military career, finishing as a Lieutenant Colonel. I directed the residency program in the family practice unit at Madigan Army hospital in Tacoma,

Washington. I also started a teaching fellowship between Pacific Lutheran University and the University of Washington. When I got out of the military, I started in private practice. I began by seeing three patients a day. I ended up seeing so many patients that I had to close my practice to new ones.

I always felt like the pushback, if you will, is not what other people give you. It's what you, yourself, believe you can't do. If you assume you can do something, you just do it, and yes, there will always be objections. They may be because you're a woman. They may be because of somebody else's ego. Who knows? None of that matters. All that matters is that you keep working, keep challenging yourself. You don't need other people to give you the right to do something. You have to give yourself the right to try.

The issue isn't how good you think you are. That's not the question you should be asking yourself. The question should be, "What do I want to do that will give me a sense of satisfaction, of having accomplished something?" Then you'll work hard at it.

People talk about living your passion, following your passion…. When you're young, you don't even know what the options are, but you do have a vague idea of what you perceive as a challenge. Go after that.

I look at my professional career and I was kind of a ten-year person. After ten years, I think there's a chance to fall into ruts. I don't like ruts. I like something to be difficult because it's a challenge. Then, when you do it anyway, you can say, "Guess what? I could do that!"

If I had not done the hard thing, I wouldn't have gotten all of the education that I got, and I wouldn't have been able to help all of the people that I helped. My real passion was not, "Oh, I want to be a doctor so I can make a lot of money." It was, "I want to help people. I want to be of service. So, what are my gifts that will enable me to be of service?" There was definitely some brash sassiness in there as well, for sure, but the only reason I could sass like I did was because I was a good student.

And that's actually why they accepted me under those circumstances. They knew me. They had seen me as a graduate student. Could I have gotten away with that in a conversation with a perfect stranger? No, probably not. But that's also a question of being able to read people and have an understanding of where they're coming from. Did I know that they probably were looking for women to enroll in medical school? No, actually I didn't. It never occurred to me. It also never occurred to me that they might reject me because I was a woman. That would have seemed very odd to me because I can't imagine a dumber basis for rejection. The fact that at that time, they had a program for reaching out to women of course worked to my advantage; I just didn't know about it.

I certainly had experiences in medical school where I was confronted by men not liking having a woman medical student. I was confronted very pointedly, in very unpleasant language. My response was mostly to ignore it and if they got too rough, I would make a big scene publicly about the fact that I was paying as much money as the male students for my education.

You just keep working as hard as you can and doing as good a job as you can. The reason is simple: a lot of people don't try that hard. If your area is mostly male, then a lot of those men are not working up to full capacity. When you are, it will be recognized. If you are productive in your field, somebody is going to want you and they are going to want to advance you, regardless of whether you are male or female. That is how change happens: one woman at a time."

"My mother told me to be a lady. And for her, that meant be your own person, be independent."
Ruth Bader Ginsburg, Supreme Court Justice

DARE TO DREAM

"Hope plays in dreams, in imagination, and in the courage of those who dare to make dreams into reality."
Jonas Salk, polio vaccine researcher

For fifteen years, my team at Let's Pretend Entertainment communicated to hundreds of thousands of people each year one passionate message: "The power of imagination is the power to change the world." How big is your imagination? Do you dare to dream big or does fear hold you back? Before you can change the world, you may need to improve your vision. Without clarity of vision, you cannot move forward in any significantly meaningful way. With clarity of vision, you can move mountains.

Since 1999, my professional job title has been Chief Daydreamer. I take responsibility for dreaming big and doing the hard work to make it happen. Too often, people avoid big dreams because they lack faith. What does faith have to do with it? Big dreams require big faith in yourself, in others, and in something much bigger than you. Call that God, the universe, or something else—when you have faith, miracles happen. Mighty forces will conspire on your behalf to create extraordinary impact in the lives of others.

Take the first step. Believe in yourself and your ability to get it done. When you don't fully believe in yourself first, you will imagine far too small. Your clouded vision can't see beyond where you currently sit, and that will hold you where you are.

You are a badass. Believe it. Own it.

Identify all the extraordinary ways in which you are a badass. Write in a journal or make a list and post it on your bathroom mirror. Review your notes every day until you know it by heart, until you believe deep down in your soul that you are highly capable and unstoppable.

Now, go out and do something really hard. Take on a challenge that stretches you beyond your boundaries. Of course, the definition of "really hard" changes from one person to the next and at different times of life. Only you can decide.

Since 2009, my company has operated on a culture of "Living 5 Rules." I believe in these rules so much, I apparently rambled about them to nurses in the ICU. You can find the list of all five rules at the end of the book, but the one to note here is Rule #4, "Do the hard thing." By continually challenging yourself to do the hard thing, you build confidence in your capacity to handle whatever comes your way.

At twenty-three years old, after I had graduated college with a bachelor's degree in Philosophy and spent a year living on little more than jello, I went to work on a fishing boat in the Bering sea off the coast of Alaska. For a year and a half, I worked twelve to fifteen hours a day, round the clock, seven days a week, in freezing cold temperatures, surrounded by dead, smelly fish. I battled systemic sexism, bone-tired fatigue, and repeated injuries. It was definitely hard. But they paid me a lot of money, enough to go back to school for another bachelor's degree, this time in Theatre. My struggles at sea taught me, deep down in my soul, that I am far tougher than I or anyone else had ever imagined.

What you know about yourself matters more than what others think about you.

Later in life, the mountains called so I started climbing. I had never even been a hiker, but one day I decided I wanted to climb mountains. We're not talking about Mt. Everest or anything similarly impressive (I'm not that badass), but it pushed my limits. After training for more than a year and hauling a fifty-pound backpack up and down several smaller peaks, my brother and I summited Mount Hood in Oregon at 11,250' and, on my fortieth birthday, Mount Rainier in Washington state at 14,411'. Just to prove I could.

Six years later in a hospital—after my pelvis had been pulverized—doctors wanted me to stand up out of the bed I had been laying in, round the clock, for fifty-five consecutive days. It was in that moment of excruciating pain that I knew why I had sailed oceans and climbed mountains. Those adventures had tested my mettle and taught me to believe in myself. I could bear whatever life threw at me, even the unbearable.

In a darkly comical twist, I am an actual literal badass. All of my gluteal muscles on the left side were amputated in an emergency lifesaving surgery when I developed sepsis after three weeks in the hospital ICU. Yet regardless of chronic pain and disabilities, I refuse to live a crippled life.

There is nothing special about me, not at all.

Imagine who you can be. Imagine what you can accomplish. What legacy can you, or do you want to leave in this world that will make it a better place for yourself and others? Challenge your capabilities. If I can do it, you absolutely can too. You just have to start dreaming. Discover your true mettle. With big vision and badass toughness, nothing can stand in your way.

"A dream doesn't become reality through magic;
it takes sweat, determination and hard work."
Colin Powell, retired four-star general

GIVE YOUR FULL ATTENTION

"It's very easy to get caught up in everything that's going on and just daily stuff being a distraction. When you have all that taken away from you, your daily activity becomes a lot more subtle, and you appreciate it all a lot more."
Tony Stewart, NASCAR racer

*H*ow many times have you sat with someone and, although they are right there, you can feel the detachment? Perhaps you said or thought, "You are a million miles away."

How often have you had a conversation with someone while their head is on a swivel or distracted by something more interesting on their phone? Your brain screams for their attention, "I'm right here!" but they aren't there, even as they speak to you. They are looking for the next opportunity, or a bigger fish, or an escape from the conversation.

Have you been alone in the quiet and, even then, unable to feel present? Your thoughts race a million miles away and the uncomfortable conversation you can't escape is the chatter of your own conflicted thoughts.

During the seven weeks I spent in an ICU, I discovered the power of presence in a way that I never before understood. Unable to move or speak, I would open my eyes to see a member of my family and, in that moment, I gave all of my presence to them. All of the energy and attention I could muster, I directed to them to silently say, "I'm here. I'm scared, but I'm still here." Everything in me was focused on being fully alive in that moment.

I could feel their full presence, there with me, without words exchanged or even eye contact. I experienced my husband simply sitting with me, every ounce of his energy focused on my wellbeing. Sure, he looked at the machines or talked to nurses, but he was fully present with me. My mother, a physician who could have easily been distracted by her too-detailed knowledge of the risks, sat holding my hand to simply assure me that I wasn't alone.

And we were all fully present with God. We begged for the presence of the Divine and were rewarded with power and peace in a way none of us had ever previously experienced. I drank in the intimacy and immediacy of all this presence as if I was dying of thirst and this was the last glass of water on earth. It was truly wondrous.

You don't need to experience massive tragedy to

understand presence. Take a moment to think through the past week, or month, or year. When was the last time you experienced someone fully present with you? When was the last time you gave someone the gift of your presence? And when did you last ask for spiritual presence in any given moment? If you can picture it, I bet it will make you smile.

Presence forges a connection outside of the ordinary. In a relationship, it makes all the difference in the world. It is the difference between life and death. I don't mean the difference between heartbeat and no heartbeat; I mean the difference between viable and not viable.

Giving or receiving undivided attention and compassionate focus grows a relationship as fast and reliably as new grass grows after a spring rain. The relationship becomes strong and viable.

The next time you are with a family member, friend, colleague, or just alone with your own spinning thoughts—slow down, take a breath, focus all of your energy and attention on *being* fully in that moment. Set aside your overrated multi-tasking ways and allow the power of presence to work miracles.

"The most precious gift we can offer anyone is our attention.
When mindfulness embraces those we love,
they will bloom like flowers."
Thich Nhat Hanh, Buddhist monk

PRACTICE PATIENCE

"Patience and fortitude conquer all things."
Ralph Waldo Emerson, poet and essayist

W e were certain my brother would be my kidney donor. Even though we didn't yet have a surgery date, we assumed it would move forward. He tested as a good match; it was just up to the surgeons to review. We cleared our calendars and prepared for hospitalization. In late July of 2015, I told at least a couple of dozen people that I would likely get a kidney transplant in August. I turned down work opportunities.

But when my brother uncharacteristically showed up at my house in the middle of his workday, I quietly knew something had gone horribly wrong. We went to Jamba Juice for smoothies, everything happy and light.

We sat on my deck in the sunshine. Dropping his gaze, he quietly uttered, "I have bad news." After months of tests and jumping through hoops, the transplant team at University of Washington had called Matt to say they weren't comfortable with the level of risk associated with putting his kidney in my trauma-scarred body. Unlike ninety-nine percent of the rest of the population that has one artery supplying blood to each kidney, my brother has three arteries supplying blood to his left kidney and four arteries supplying blood to his right kidney. To perform this type of rare transplant is difficult in the best of circumstances, but in my body it was likely impossible.

I tried to get my head around this disappointment. What would this mean? For seven months I had been living without dialysis by radically restricting my diet. The access port for dialysis had been removed due to infection risk. Every week after having blood drawn for tests, I held my breath. Kidney function was down to twelve percent. It could easily plummet and plunge me once again into a life-threatening emergency. I would have to wait until we could find transplant surgeons experienced with highly complex cases like mine. "Hang on Elisa," I tried to assure myself. "Just keep hanging on."

Before meeting up with my brother that day, I had spoken at a Toastmasters meeting about "Living 5 Rules." Rule #5, "Play the long game," is all about setting a vision and having the patience to see it through. I had no idea how ironically appropriate the reminder would be that day. On the way home from the meeting, just before encountering my brother, road construction blocked my usual route. A large warning sign blinked, "EXPECT DELAYS" — spelled just like that. I chuckled out loud, "Apparently there was a delay in fifth grade English!" Altogether, I felt very clever. A common problem of mine.

After talking with Matt, it was clear I should indeed expect delays. Life is like that. We think we have all the answers. We've worked out the plan in our heads and scoff at the warning signs. We are too clever for our own good sometimes.

Practice patience, darling.

My brother and I didn't give up; eventually we found the best solution possible, but it did take patience.

The University of Maryland Medical Center in Baltimore agreed to take our case. In the early pre-dawn of September 1, 2015, Matt and I were prepped for surgery. Dr. Stephen Bartlett, the hospital's Chief Medical Officer and a microvascular surgeon with experience in rare multiple renal artery transplants, reviewed our reality in no-nonsense terms, "We'll take Elisa into the operating room, open her up and, if we think we can do it, then we'll take Matt in to remove his left kidney. If it doesn't look good, we'll just close her back up."

Nine hours later, I opened my eyes to my husband's

sweet face. "Do I have a kidney?" I groggily asked. "Yes, you do. It worked," he answered with a big smile.

*"It's not that I'm so smart, it's just that
I stay with problems longer."*
Albert Einstein

DON'T TAKE YOURSELF TOO SERIOUSLY

"If you find it hard to laugh at yourself,
I would be happy to do it for you."
Groucho Marx, actor and comedian

*A*fter having an organ transplant, the recipient must take immunosuppressive medication for the rest of their life to prevent rejection. Hand washing and vaccinations take on a whole other level of importance. Before getting a new kidney, I researched which vaccines I would need. The shingles vaccine recommended for everyone over age sixty was a "live" vaccine (unlike the newer one developed since) and not allowed after a transplant. I was only forty-eight years old. It took some convincing, but our insurance agreed to pay for the vaccine before my transplant since I wouldn't be able to have it after-wards. Woohoo! I got the shingles vaccine and proceeded to transplant feeling both safer and smarter.

Fast forward ten months…. It turned out I didn't know everything. Shocker. The shingles vaccine, while important, was only fifty-one percent effective, and less so in immune-compromised people such as organ transplant recipients—like me. After four days of suffering brutal rib and back pain, I woke up on a Monday morning with a garish rash wrapping in a wide swath around the right side of my ribs from spine to sternum. Twenty-four hours later, the tell-tale blisters appeared.

Fortunately, I had a doctor appointment scheduled that day and was able to get started on the antiviral medication immediately. He also gave me pain pills and lidocaine patches to numb the skin. My bedroom looked like a pharmacy, but once again I felt smart. Briefly.

After twenty-four hours of aggressively managing pain with pharmaceuticals, wine, and chocolate, I finally read the directions on the prescription lidocaine patches, out of curiosity. After all, how complicated could it be? Peel off the backing and stick the patch to your skin. What else is there to know? "Do not use for more than twelve hours in a twenty-four-hour period." Huh.

Husband: "How long have you been wearing the patches?"

Me: "Twenty-four hours. I've been in hellish pain!"

Husband: "Yeah, getting too much lidocaine in your system is bad."

Me: "Why? Does it make you go numb inside?"

Husband stares blankly….

It turns out that too much lidocaine absorbed through the skin can be fatal. I can just see the obituary —"She died from a sticker."

If you can't be smart, at least be funny. Especially about your own silly awkwardness.

Maybe you have felt pretty smart at times. And maybe you have had your pride knocked down a peg or two. Much like shingles, it hurts. How we react makes all the difference. As long as you don't get angry and defensive, these humbling lessons provide rich opportunities to add useful knowledge and humorous anecdotes to your toolkit. You never know when those tools could be a lifesaver.

"If you can laugh at yourself, you are going to be fine.
If you allow others to laugh with you, you will be great."
Martin Niemöller, theologian

YOU ALREADY HAVE WHAT
YOU NEED

*"Everything you need you already have. You are complete
right now, you are a whole, total person, not an apprentice
person on the way to someplace else. Your completeness must
be understood by you and experienced in your thoughts as
your own personal reality."*
Wayne Dyer, author

Shortly after getting married, my husband and
I worked as actors for a woman who owned a
children's show called Let's Pretend Circus. We traveled to Washington, Oregon, California, and Hawaii
performing the audience participation show at fairs. It
was a fun gig! But then we wanted to have children of
our own. It was time to get a so-called real job.

Three years later, in the spring of 1999, the owner
of Let's Pretend Circus called offering to sell the show

to us. She explained that she was getting out of the business; Steve and I were the best who had ever worked for her—obviously—and she wanted to sell her business to us for the incredible bargain of $5,000. Great! Except we didn't have $5,000.

We discussed it and concluded we could offer her half the money down and the balance after completing a contract that she already had in place with a client for the fall. She would probably take that offer. Except we didn't have $2,500. We were young and broke.

One morning, about a week later, I went to a Bible study for moms at church and shared our dilemma with the women in the group. Together, we prayed about it. Afterward, I went out to my car, buckled my two-year-old and nine-month-old in their car seats, and headed for home. During the entire fifteen-minute drive, I heard a voice in my head emphatically repeating, "I've already given you the money. I've already given you the money." It was insistent. For the record, it wasn't out loud. I have many problems, but schizophrenia isn't one of them. The voice definitely wasn't my own mind, either, because my out loud response was, "What money? If I had $2,500, I would know it!" Over and over again, insistently, "I've already given you the money. I've already given you the money." By the time I arrived home, I had attributed the voice to God. And I still had no idea what money I was already supposed to have.

Sitting in my car at the house with the engine running, all of a sudden, a cartoon light bulb went off over my head. Okay not really, but it sure felt like it.

Three years prior, when I was pregnant with our oldest child, my best friend, Billy, died of AIDS at twenty-nine years old. This was during the height of the AIDS epidemic, before the discovery of medications presently available that could have prolonged his life. A month after his funeral in South Dakota, I received a letter in the mail from his mom. She shared details from his will and added, "Billy always wanted to take care of you." Enclosed was a check for $2,500. I had solemnly put the money into a mutual fund and intentionally forgotten about it...until that very moment.

Jumping out of the car, I ran into the house screaming, "God wants us to buy a circus!"

That $2,500 became the seed money for a business that grew over the next fifteen years as Let's Pretend Entertainment, with multiple teams of performers crisscrossing the continent. I had already been given what I needed well in advance because God knew what was coming long before I did.

Facing the future can be intimidating. Thankfully, you don't have to know how everything is going to work out.

Believe in yourself and trust in God. You may not know it now, but you have already been given what you need.

"You can't connect the dots looking forward; you can only connect them looking backwards. So you have to trust that the dots will somehow connect in your future. You have to

trust in something—your gut, destiny, life, karma, whatever. This approach has never let me down, and it has made all the difference in my life."
Steve Jobs, cofounder of Apple Computers

EMBRACE TRUE BEAUTY

"What sort of sap doesn't know by now that picture-perfect beauty is all done with smoke and mirrors anyway?"
Julie Burchill, journalist

*H*ave you ever noticed that women will shop for fabulous clothes, not to impress men, but to impress other women? It's how we establish our power structure. Who is prettier? Who has higher cheekbones? Who has a better butt (definitely not me)? The pretty girls get more things and more attention. They get special perks just for being pretty. Some young women head out into the world as a "professional" but being pretty is the sharpest tool in their tool belt. That can't last long. We've all seen the sad situation of a middle-aged woman acting like a college co-ed. From there, it leads to fighting aging, as if it is somehow the devil, instead of embracing that women can be beautiful at any age. It all stems from miscon-struing true beauty.

You are smart, capable, tough, and kind. And that is what makes you beautiful.

Don't misunderstand. There's no reason to dress sloppy or intentionally avoid good grooming. Dress nicely. Put on makeup. Fix your hair. Those are good things, but they are a bonus, like the ornaments on a Christmas tree. They're decorative, not structural. The real structure that will elevate you in the world depends on being smart, capable, tough, and kind.

Some people have the misguided idea that there are "the smart girls" and then "the pretty girls," as if those are mutually exclusive. They are not. Maybe you don't consider yourself pretty, but that false belief beats up your self-esteem. When you beat up your self-esteem, you diminish your capacity for being capable and tough. And damaging your self-esteem definitely isn't kind.

True beauty comes from your personal presence, not from your dress size, from your kindness, not from batting your eyelashes. Coming back to the Christmas tree analogy—all of the ornaments in the world won't make an ugly tree more beautiful. You, who you are as a person, are the tree and the true source of beauty.

When you feel genuinely confident in yourself, you can go into the professional world and be tough, an essential, without being mean. Some women believe that to play in a man's world, you have to act like a bitch. Not true. Although sometimes women who need to make tough choices are called that or worse. It is unfortunately true that a woman can act just like a man and she will be called names, while he is respected. It is equally true that some women behave badly because they've confused toughness with harshness. For example, you might have to fire somebody, but that doesn't mean you need to be cruel. You can still be kind and gentle in difficult conversations.

Gentleness is often considered a feminine quality and equated with weakness. It's not. If you have acted with compassion in a difficult circumstance, you've done the hard thing. True mental fortitude requires enough self-control to maintain gentleness, and nothing can be tougher. What will elevate you in the workplace is your ability to solve problems, persevere, be creative, and communicate in ways that motivate and inspire others to be of service. Exercise compassion, kindness, humility, and gentleness. Whether or not you have long eyelashes and can rock skinny jeans is irrelevant.

You can't flirt your way into professional success.

Will adorableness work for a little while? Yes. When you're twenty-three. But it's a lot less cute when you're thirty-five or forty. Why keep practicing the skill you learned when you were five years old? Look at photos of little girls getting their picture taken; it's weirdly common to see them put their hand on their hip, tilt their head, grin coyly, and flash a twinkle in their eye.

That skill gets practiced over and over and over because, let's be honest, to a certain point it works.

Many girls grow up having that skill finely developed. Then they get out in the professional world and it's all they know how to do. I've seen it. I employed and mentored lots of young women who had mastered that skillset. Many women haven't practiced leadership skills that will advance them very far in their career. They've learned how to be little girls, not women. A professional woman in the world is smart, capable, tough, and may very well happen to be pretty.

"Women have made tons of progress. But we still have a small percentage of the top jobs in any industry, in any nation in the world. I think that's partly because from a very young age, we encourage our boys to lead and we call our girls bossy."
Sheryl Sandberg, Chief Operating Officer of Facebook

GET COURAGEOUSLY REAL

"Always be yourself. Everyone else is already taken."
Oscar Wilde, playwright

*I*f you want to make everything perfect and do it "right," you aren't alone. Research shows that perfectionism, particularly among young adults, has risen significantly. Along with it, anxiety and depression have also risen. The problem with trying to do everything perfectly is that you can't. You will find it incredibly hard, time consuming, energy draining, and sooner or later, you will fail.

Yet movies, TV, magazines, and social media fill our brains with expectations of how a "good girl" should look, act, talk, and feel. The 1980 Enjoli television commercial, designed to sell perfume, presents an absurd distortion of the 1970s feminist movement that still encapsulates the ideal against which many women feel measured. And which many men naively expect.

"I can bring home the bacon." Perfect career professional.
"Fry it up in a pan." Perfect domestic goddess.
"And never, ever, ever let you forget you're a man." Perfect sex symbol and attentive wife. Yuck.

My goodness, that is exhausting! When you try to fit yourself into a preconceived mold of who you imagine people expect you to be, you miss out on who you really are. You present a figment of yourself. No matter how good your acting chops, pretending will never be real. I've been on stages around the globe since I was four years old as a dancer, actor, entertainer, and speaker. I've done a lot of performing in my life, acting as though I had everything perfectly under control when that couldn't have been further from the truth.

Most of us go through large portions of our lives acting, pretending we know what we're doing. What we really do is edit. So much of your real personality lands on a metaphorical cutting room floor. You decide what doesn't fit with the image you try to portray. I'm not suggesting you blurt out every thought that comes through your head. That could get you in a lot of trouble and hurt others. Besides, blurting isn't authenticity. In today's fast-paced, pop-culture world, authenticity frequently gets confused with bad manners. You know those folks who pridefully espouse, "I just tell it like it is!"

Yuck. Genuine authenticity means aligning your speech and actions with your values. You show up, in all circumstances, true to who you really are. You are enough. You don't need a shined up, fictional characterization of you.

Put your best self out into the world, of course. But don't try to pretend perfection. By hiding our humanity, we project the message to others that they must hide theirs. Relationships drown in the shallow end of the pool.

When you show up honestly—with all of your aspirations, fears, hopes, failings, awkwardness, and anxieties—you show up as a real person. You give others permission to do the same. It's scary and rare, but worth it.

When I was in college, I neglected to write a paper for a class. (Possibly more than once, but this isn't *True Confessions*.) I went to this particular professor and said, "You may have noticed, I didn't turn in the paper. If I turn it in tomorrow, will I receive any credit?" Simple enough question. We stood outside the big brick building that housed the Philosophy department on a beautiful sunny Pacific Northwest day. I smiled pleasantly and awaited his answer.

He looked at me for a long minute. When it became clear I wasn't saying anything further he asked flatly, "Do you have a reason? Were you sick?"

"No, I just didn't feel like writing it yet."

The ethics professor stammered, "Are you kidding?

Don't you want to lie to me? Your dog died or...something?"

I shrugged, "Why? Would you grade me better if I lied to you?"

Grinning broadly, he said, "Well okay then. With an answer like that, you can turn it in tomorrow for full credit." He walked off shaking his head in disbelief.

I took the risk and was willing to take the hit because being true to myself and others was more important than lying to get a better grade. I have definitely not always been so noble, but I've never forgotten that moment. It showed me the petty commonness of dishonesty.

Don't be common.

Whatever you do, be real. Be true to yourself, even if it means taking the hit for it. That is authentic.

> *"Honesty and transparency make you vulnerable.*
> *Be honest and transparent anyway."*
> *Mother Teresa, Saint Teresa of Calcutta*

JUST DO IT

"I attribute my success to this:
I never gave or took any excuse."
Florence Nightingale, social reformer

*F*lorence Nightingale, born in 1820, was widely considered the founder of modern nursing. She's also one of the earliest feminists. Nurses rock!

In 1867, she declared herself for women's suffrage —the right to vote, which was considered highly controversial during the Victorian era. She lived in the United Kingdom and, unfortunately, died eighteen years before all women received the same voting rights as men.

About a year after she died, on March 8, 1911, International Women's Day was marked for the first time by over a million people in Austria, Denmark,

Germany, and Switzerland. Notice not the United States, nor the UK. In America, the nineteenth amendment guaranteeing all women the right to vote wasn't ratified until August 18, 1920.

Never take for granted your right to vote.

For years, every November I sat with my kids to watch the movie *Iron Jawed Angels*, about the suffragist fight in America. Full disclosure, they didn't have a vote in whether or not to watch it with me. It might take us three hours to finish the movie, even when I already knew what happens, because I would frequently pause the film to rant. —"Don't ever miss a chance a vote!" and "Always be the one who will fight for the rights of those without a voice." I highly recommend you watch that extraordinarily good movie.

It took until 1975 for the United Nations to adopt International Women's Day. It is now celebrated every year on the eighth of March, commemorating the women's rights movement. It is also known as United Nations Day for Women's Rights and International Peace.

Women such as Florence Nightingale and other suffragists had to fight for men to give them their rights. Now, the bigger problem is not that women need to fight for it; it's that women need to step up and claim it.

If you want to see more women in leadership, than *be* in leadership. As Florence Nightingale said, she never gave or took any excuse. I hate to quote Nike, but "Just Do It." Go get it. Be like Florence Nightingale.

Press for progress by stepping up boldly and leading the way.

Remember that the leadership you want and deserve doesn't come by being aggressive. Very rarely does it come by fighting. It comes by using your voice and your presence. It comes by using your confidence. That is how you press for progress. Does that mean great disparities in the workplace don't exist? No, they really do. Unfortunately, women today still make up only 18 percent of the top C-suite level employees, with women of color holding only 3 percent. This, by the way, is an improvement.

I will still firmly maintain that in today's era, the best way for progress is not made by fighting others, but by living your confidence. Your belief in who you are and what you can do is far more important and more impactful than any ideas the world could ever give you about your limitations. So, neither give for yourself, nor accept from yourself, any excuses. That doesn't mean be unkind; it means have fortitude.

"People spend too much time finding other people to blame, too much energy finding excuses for not being what they are capable of being, and not enough energy putting themselves on the line, growing out of the past, and getting on with their lives."
J. Michael Straczynski, screenwriter and producer

SPEAK WITH HEART

"According to most studies, people's number one fear is public speaking. Number two is death. Death is number two. Does that seem right? That means to the average person, if you have to go to a funeral, you're better off in the casket than doing the eulogy."
Jerry Seinfeld, comedian

I recall sitting outside on the back deck of our house with our youngest daughter, Sarah. She was talking about how intimidating public speaking is. What I do professionally, most people fear pathologically. A few lucky talkers just seem wired this way from the womb. I started talking at ten months old, and never stopped.

According to several studies, the fear of public speaking (glossophobia) has been listed as the number one fear. As of 2018, the US population totaled 327.2

million. Six percent of male Americans (approximately 9.8 million) and 8 percent of female Americans (approximately 13 million) struggle with speaking anxiety. Isn't it interesting that so many more women than men fear using their voice in public settings?

When you don't speak up, your opinions and expertise never get shared. Your knowledge, wisdom, and curiosity are never heard. Your compassion and kindness are never seen. What a mighty loss to the world.

Your voice matters.

What if you genuinely appreciate the power of using your voice, but you're still terrified to get up in front of an audience of people? What can we do about that? Old conventional wisdom would tell you to picture the audience in their underwear. I suppose if that helps, then knock yourself out and enjoy the view! Other conventional wisdom would say to look over the tops of their heads; the audience won't know any different. They won't be able to tell. The problem with that advice is they actually can. People can always tell what isn't real. You can't fake it.

Some folks would tell you to script yourself and memorize it verbatim or use note cards. Have you watched speakers like that? It's painful. Seriously. Really painful.

In all my years coaching performers and speakers at every level of experience, the first principle people fail to understand is the importance of speaking with heart. Your voice and your heart are so intrinsically tied that it is exactly why you feel afraid to speak in public.

When you use your voice, your heart becomes vulnerable. Risk it anyway. Open your heart before you open your mouth.

As you look at the audience, genuinely care about the people. We get stage fright because we focus on ourselves. Your heart becomes vulnerable when you use your voice. You fear people will be unimpressed, or worse, and that risks hurting your heart. The best way to practice comfort in front of an audience is to practice vulnerability. When speaking to one person...or two or three, can you be real? Can you look at them and care genuinely about their wellbeing?

Now for the next important piece: You need complete confidence that they need what you have to say. If you talk strictly for the purpose of marketing or branding, or because it's an assignment and you have to, then it will be painful for you and them. When you speak with confidence, not vain arrogance, you can genuinely give value and assistance.

Value your voice and be vulnerable with your heart. Then you can speak to audiences of any size, whether one person or one thousand. It won't matter because they will feel and recognize your genuine care for them. When you look out at the audience and see people, individuals with all of the vulnerable messiness of being human, it becomes easier to use your voice. You can make a difference for them. You have so many things to share with the world. People need to hear you.

> *"It took me quite a long time to develop a voice, and now that I have it, I am not going to be silent."*
> *Madeleine Albright, former British Prime Minister*

DAYDREAM

"Everything starts as somebody's daydream."
Larry Niven, science fiction author

*A*ccording to *Inc. Magazine*, "The average person rarely considers how ordinary things can be made better or improved; those with the entrepreneurial spirit can't help themselves." Upon first reading that, I laughed and recalled envisioning improvements in the hospital environment. Did you know a portable x-ray machine could be redesigned to look like a cartoon snail? Or that institutional beige vertical blinds could be transformed into swaying eighteenth-century dancers? Both true. And I swear I wasn't on pain medicine when I imagined it. The world is full of potential for whimsical improvement! Foster in yourself a creative, entrepreneurial spirit. It is badly needed by many organizations and individuals struggling to push progress.

Thinking creatively means allowing your mind to connect seemingly unrelated dots. Do you remember, as a little kid, watching clouds and seeing shapes? "That one looks like an elephant!" Most adults lose the ability to see something for anything except what we know it to be. That limitation clogs thinking and stalls creative problem solving.

Build your imagination as a part of your daily habits like brushing your teeth and putting on underwear.

Try starting with a simple doodling game for exercising creative muscles: Grab a pencil and paper. Close your eyes and scribble randomly. If you need structure, set a timer for one minute. Open your eyes. Look at your "art" and write down all the different things that you see in the picture. This may require some big leaps of imagination. Making cloud-shape type comparisons is known as metaphorical thinking, a critical component of creativity.

Now push the paper aside and go do something else. Later in the day, grab the paper and look again. Turn it different ways in front of you. Hold it at a distance. Try tilting it at different angles. What else do you see this time? Creativity requires resting the brain. During that incubation period, neurons continue to make connections in the background while your frontal lobe works on tasks at hand.

Remember lazy summer days laying in the grass watching clouds? You were relaxed, unhurried, and playful—not at all stressed, busy, and hyper-productive. Counter-intuitively, to dream up creative solutions to grown-up problems, we need to think like kids just watching clouds.

"I think kids are natural actors. You watch most kids; if they don't have a toy, they'll pick up a stick and make a toy out of it. Kids will daydream all the time."
Clint Eastwood, actor and filmmaker

GIVE GRACE

"Empathy is simply listening, holding space, withholding judgment, emotionally connecting, and communicating that incredibly healing message of you're not alone."
Brené Brown, PhD, researcher

Several years ago, one of my employees had to do what every employee dreads most. She had to call her boss to confess that she did something wrong. Prior to the offense, I had told her not to do the exact thing that she ended up doing [sigh]. She drove a company truck, a three-quarter-ton diesel Ford, into a parking garage in downtown Seattle…and got it stuck. After a lot of scratching and scraping, she managed to back out of the entrance to the parking garage, but not without damage to the roof of the truck. My truck.

In moments such as this, those who aspire to leadership are faced with a decision. Whether at home with your family or in the workplace with colleagues, the immediate temptation can be to play the shame card. We want to teach them a lesson and ensure that it never happens again, right?

Pause. Take a slow breath. Widen your perspective.

Imagine the panic, fear, guilt, and many more emotions my team member was already feeling as she pulled out her phone to dial her boss's number. She was about to own up to a mistake that would certainly cost the company financially and could cost her position within the company. At the very least, it would cost her trustworthiness in the eyes of her boss. Can you imagine that feeling in your gut?

When I received that phone call and heard what happened, instead of reacting reflexively, I took a deep breath and gathered my composure. I paused long enough to put myself in her shoes. Once there, I knew she had already learned her lesson. No amount of shame and blame from me would improve the outcome. I simply replied, "We will take care of it."

Wording is a funny thing. Respond with "we" instead of "you" and trust goes up dramatically.

By choosing empathy instead of blame, you set a tone of togetherness and build a culture of compassion. Questions such as, "What knowledge have you gained from this experience?" and, "How will this experience help you in the future?" nurture an environment that values growth, positive impact, and empathy rather than harsh criticism, shame, isolation, and punishment.

To build a strong community of people around you, rein in your reactivity. Learn to increase the gap between input and response so you have that split-second of time to gather your composure. By responding with thoughtful, empathic grace, you demonstrate that you can be trusted to treat others with dignity, even with all their flaws. In return, they are much more likely to give grace to you when you need it, as you most surely will.

"The ideal man (woman) bears the accidents of life with dignity and grace, making the best of circumstances."
Aristotle, philosopher

ACTUALLY CARE

"People don't care how much you know
until they know how much you care."
Attributed to Theodore Roosevelt, Zig Ziglar,
John Maxwell, and others.
It's simply a truism.

*I*n early 2018, in response to a news scandal, Starbucks announced they would close 8,000 stores for half a day to conduct racial bias training for 175,000 employees. Two black men in a Philadelphia Starbucks had asked to use the restroom. They were told the restroom was for paying customers so they would need to buy something. Okay, no problem. They sat down. While sitting without incident, they were told they needed to buy something or leave the store. They replied that they were waiting to meet someone at the store. The manager called the police, complaining that two men in the store refused to either buy product or leave. Police came and arrested the men. They weren't violent, aggressive, or even particularly confrontational. In fact, a crowd of witnesses were yelling, "What have they done? They've done nothing wrong!" As you can imagine, phones came out and the whole scene was video recorded. It went viral all over the Internet.

In the same week national news was occupied with the negative customer experience at Starbucks, I was filming a warm, customer appreciation video at the request of one of their district managers. The video showed me at home, buying coffee at a drive-through, and going into a store in my wheelchair. The message was that as a Pacific Northwest native who travels all over the world, buying coffee at Starbucks has always felt like a little bit of home. I've been in thirty-three states and twenty countries to date; every time I go to Starbucks it feels warm and friendly, like home.

How I became connected to the Starbucks district manager for whom I made the video is an interesting story. While in my wheelchair, trying to buy coffee at a licensed store in the Phoenix airport, I had an unfortunate experience. I made a video about that too. My negative experience went minor viral. Starbucks corporate got wind of it. The district manager overseeing licensed stores in that region contacted me to learn more about the experience and discern what could be improved. We've since become friends and I've had wonderful experiences, but when I told him about my experience in my wheelchair, I expressed this was not a disability issue. I wasn't making an ADA complaint; this was a human issue. They don't need disability awareness training so much as they need empathy training.

Implicit or unconscious biases are preconceptions you don't realize you have because they act beneath the level of your awareness. The unconscious biases that create gaps in customer service and inclusive experiences at work and play (gender, ability, race, age, politics, and more) are fueled by one common denominator—a lack of empathy. We don't need more "awareness" training. We need more empathy. The problem with closing 8,000 corporate stores for an afternoon of racial bias training is that it's not really a racial issue. It manifested in this particular circumstance as a racial issue, but at the heart of it is actually a lack of empathy. It's about seeing people, caring, listening, and connecting genuinely.

People need attention and presence. You have to take time to actually care. People need to feel they have been seen and heard. They may not get exactly what they want out of the circumstance, but the outcome will often improve tremendously if they feel you care.

"I'm right, you're wrong, and my point of view matters more." That's really the bias we *all* have. Everyone falls prey to an ugly, egocentric belief that almost nobody admits, "How I feel trumps how you feel. In fact, I don't actually care how you feel." Get really honest with yourself. Then you can change. Then you can actually care.

In "awareness training" people learn all the right things to say. The problem with teaching people to say practiced phrases that sound as if they care, when in fact they don't, is that it simply doesn't work. Human beings are pretty good lie detectors.

W.C. Fields reportedly asserted he would never perform with children or animals because they will always command focus on a stage. Children and animals are 100 percent real every single time. Our brains are wired to give attention to that which is most real. Think about it. YouTube videos of puppies are far more endearing than somebody trying to act like a puppy. That's just dumb.

The same is true when it comes to dealing with people, whether it is an issue of customer service, leadership, or a personal relationship. If you don't genuinely care, people will know you're faking. There's only one way to convey that you actually care and can set aside feelings and focus on facts—empathy. That's it.

Pause and put yourself in another person's shoes.

In 2009, I created "Living 5 Rules" as the guiding principles for my company, and for life in general. Rule #2 is "Actually Care." In my company, Let's Pretend Entertainment, I repeatedly reminded my team, "You have to <u>actually</u> care. No pretending allowed." Take the time to deeply listen without your inner dialogue thinking about what you will say next. Stop all the chatter in your mind and just listen. Focus on how the other person feels and reflect back your understanding. Show empathy and the results will astound you, no matter what issue is at stake.

"When you show deep empathy toward others, their defensive energy goes down, and positive energy replaces it. That's when you can get more creative in solving problems."
Stephen Covey, author

MASTER YOUR MIND LIKE A JEDI

"If your emotional abilities aren't in hand, if you don't have self-awareness, if you are not able to manage your distressing emotions, if you can't have empathy and have effective relationships, then no matter how smart you are, you are not going to get very far."
Daniel Goleman, journalist

*G*ood leaders demonstrate a high level of emotional intelligence, otherwise known as EQ. They show strong empathy, deep self-awareness, and a genuine interest in the people they lead. But *great* leaders take it to another level; they exercise emotional foresight.

In October 2016, I tripped over a drawer in my bathroom and fell. Non-climactic to say the least. That clumsy misstep earned me a free trip to the hospital Emergency Department with a gruesomely broken wrist. After returning home to sulk in bed, I called my mother. You are just never too old for your mama. A forward-thinking woman, mom promptly whipped out her phone and said, "What's on your schedule? I will clear my calendar. You're going to need someone to take you to your speaking engagements and doctor appointments." As mothers usually are, the woman was absolutely right. Severe pain radiated up my arm and into my neck for weeks. Without the use of my right hand to hold a cane, I couldn't walk more than a few steps or push my wheelchair. I could barely dress myself. That absent-minded trip over a drawer cost me nearly all of my independent mobility for two months.

From this experience, I discovered emotional fore-sight. My mother took emotional intelligence to the next level by wielding it like Yoda and foreseeing the obstacles in my path. She quickly adapted to ensure my success at her expense, activating the foundational piece of great leadership: Put others first.

To impact the lives of others, you have to look beyond the here and now. By practicing emotional foresight, you prepare for the welfare of others, ensuring that when something goes sideways, your people—whether family, friends, or colleagues at work —are protected, supported, and cared for. Practiced over time, this becomes second nature.

ASSESS Facts: Observe the situational facts and ask how it will or could impact others.

ACCEPT Reality: Let the facts just be what they are.

Don't waste time or energy on blame, anger, or avoidance.

ADDRESS Needs: Ask what it will take to create success for others? Once you know, take responsibility and put others first!

Taking EQ to a Jedi Master level requires inquiry, responsibility, and thinking ahead. When you integrate this way of thinking into the fabric of your being, there is no limit to how far you can go.

> *"It is very important to understand that emotional*
> *intelligence is not the opposite of intelligence,*
> *it is not the triumph of heart over head*
> *—it is the unique intersection of both."*
> *David Caruso, actor*

START THE DAY GENTLY

"Good habits are worth being fanatical about."
John Irving, novelist

*R*esearch has shown that the busiest, most successful leaders in the world don't dive straight into work; they begin the day with a self-care routine to get themselves grounded. If the world's busiest leaders have time for an intentional morning, surely us ordinary folk can make room in our schedules.

After the accident, when I spent most days in my bedroom, I launched a new habit of beginning my mornings with meditation, prayer, and whatever exercise or movement I was capable of doing. For a long time, making the bed was a serious form of exercise. As I've grown in strength and energy, I've become much busier; but with good habits in place, I still start the day with positive intention.

My days begin by writing in a gratitude journal, reading a Bible devotional, doing light yoga, and sitting in either a silent or guided meditation. These centering practices calm my erratic, bouncing thoughts and prepare me to focus on the day ahead.

Stop rolling your eyes. I'm a mom, so I can feel an eye roll through any amount of time and space. I'm really not saying, "Oh look how perfect I am!" In fact, starting the day by taking care of mind, body, and spirit didn't become a regular practice in my life until after I was so deeply traumatized that I had to either learn better coping skills or lose my mind. I used to just get up and mumble until I had enough coffee. Sometimes I still do that. Okay, actually, I always do that, except now I add the other practices. Then I'm ready to talk to other humans.

What about you? How do you start the day? Do you tumble out of bed, grumble about being awake, and jump straight to work? Do you flip on the television? Read the news? If you could design your mornings in any way that best fuels your engines, what would that look like?

This is your life. You get to choose.

If you need motivation to establish a routine that will build focus, try reading *The Miracle Morning* by Hal Elrod. I also highly recommend *The Five Minute Journal*, either in print or through the app. It is the easiest, fastest, most delightful way to infuse a positive attitude into any day. (I don't receive any kickback for either recommendation.)

Find whatever works for you. More than anything, simply commit to starting the day gently by nourishing your mind, body, and soul before heading off to conquer the world. You'll be more productive and happier doing it. Now that's a good morning!

"Being lazy does not mean that you do not create.
In fact, lying around doing nothing is an important,
nay crucial, part of the creative process. It is meaningless
bustle that actually gets in the way of productivity.
All we are really saying is, give peace a chance."
Tom Hodgkinson, writer

DO ONE THING AT A TIME

"You can do two things at once, but you can't focus effectively on two things at once."
Gary Keller, author

$\mathcal{E}$very one of us lives with a continuous bombardment of interruptions—phone calls, emails, texts, social media messages, people dropping by, etc., etc., rinse and repeat.

They can all seem equally important and demanding. You don't want to miss anything, disappoint someone, or fail somehow because you didn't respond fast enough to everyone at the moment they wanted it.

Is the pressure to multitask valid?

Are you allowing yourself to be trained into an A.D.D. way of living?

Are you allowing others to control your time and focus, while you train them to expect an unreasonable rate of response?

Research has shown that our brains can only focus on one thing at a time. What we call multitasking is in fact not simultaneous attention; it's rapid switching. When we hop spastically from one interruption to the next, we slow down productivity, accuracy, and—most importantly—real connection to humanity. Multitasking slows down your brain and overall effectiveness. Not to mention, it increases stress while decreasing life satisfaction.

Insist on one thing at a time.

Purposefully set your intention and focus on what the priority is right now. This moment. Protect your time and energy—it is all any of us have. Turn off your phone and TV while you're doing something else. Be bold and turn off those ever-tempting instant notifications. You're not ignoring anyone; just check notifications when it fits in with your time and ability to give full attention. Give every person and project in your life the respect of your complete focus.

It's okay to control the input in your life. We can respect the needs of others without allowing our attention to be yanked around like a leaf at the mercy of the wind.

"Multi-tasking is great in the kitchen when you are trying to time the chicken to be ready at the same time as the potatoes. But do not assume it is a great way to manage a workday."
Joanne Tombrakos, author

FAIL LIKE A WINNER

"Winning is great, sure, but if you're really going to do something in life, the secret is learning how to lose. Nobody goes undefeated ALL the time. If you can pick up after a crushing defeat and go on to win again, you are going to be a champion someday."
Wilma Rudolph, Olympic runner

Failure—the Big F. FAILURE hurts. Admitting you are human, fallible, and eminently imperfect is painful. No one likes it.

Because of disabilities and chronic pain, I'm often tired. At least once a month, I lay in bed feeling like a failure because I am simply too tired to do all the work I really want to do. I want to give up. But then a little voice in my head says, "You know you're not actually going to give up, so stop whining about it." Snarky little voice that she is.

Wilma Rudolph, born in Tennessee in 1940, made Olympic history in 1960 when she became the first American woman ever to win three gold medals in track and field events. Before winning, she had endless reasons to quit.

Wilma began life poor, black, the twentieth of twenty-two of her father's children, and born premature weighing only four and a half pounds. She spent the bulk of her childhood in bed. Wilma suffered from double pneumonia and scarlet fever, all before she turned four years old. Then she contracted polio and lost the use of her left leg. Doctors fitted her with metal leg braces when she was six and informed her family that she would wear leg braces or use a wheelchair for the rest of her life. Her quite large and wonderful family rallied to help this tiny child thrive. For five years, her mother—a housemaid—drove ninety miles roundtrip once a week to see a doctor at the big hospital in Nashville, Tennessee. She received leg treatments that involved massages multiple times a day.

At the age of nine, Wilma decided she'd had enough. To her doctor's amazement, she pulled her leg braces off and started walking! I particularly love this story because I was never expected to walk again either.

Wilma soon joined her brothers and sisters in basketball games in the back yard. By the time she was twelve years old, she was challenging every boy in the neighborhood at running and jumping. In high school, she lived for basketball; so, she joined the girls' basketball team at an all African American high school. In 1950s Tennessee, segregation was a way of life. Burt

High School had a girls' basketball team and coach Clinton Gray gave Wilma the nickname Skeeter. He said she was little, fast, and always in his way.

At fourteen, little Skeeter attracted the attention of Ed Temple, the women's track coach at Tennessee State University. He suggested Gray start a girls' track team to train some of the basketball forwards as sprinters. Who he really had in mind was Wilma. He believed she had the potential to become a great runner. And he was right.

When someone believes in you, *believe them*. Don't let low self-esteem feed you lies.

During summer breaks from high school, the poor little girl from the sticks trained with Coach Temple and the students at Tennessee State University. That was when she first learned of the Olympics. At sixteen years old, Wilma Rudolph qualified for the 1956 Summer Olympics in Melbourne, Australia. Can you imagine what that felt like for this little girl who was never expected to walk on her own? She competed as a sprinter in the Olympics and took home a bronze medal!

After Wilma got a taste of victory, she joined the university and ran herself nearly to death. From 1958 to 1959, she suffered repeated crushing illnesses and injuries from the stresses she placed on her body. Her drive to win was literally causing her failure. Through the encouragement and coaching that she received, she persevered. In 1960, Wilma became the first American woman to win three gold medals in a single Olympic Games.

At the Olympics in Rome, Italy, in both the 100-meter dash and the 200-meter dash, she finished at least three yards in front of her closest competitor. She tied the world record in the 100-meter and set a new Olympic record in the 200-meter. Wilma also brought her 400-meter relay team from behind to win the gold, despite a bad handoff of the baton. It wasn't all about her and her accomplishments. In fact, winning in the relay was Wilma's favorite because she stood on the podium with her teammates.

She became an instant celebrity throughout Europe and America. Everywhere she went, crowds gathered to see the amazing "gazelle," as the French called her. Wilma was given parades and an official invitation to the White House by President Kennedy, but she did more than revel in her celebrity status, success, and fame. She created change for other people. Wilma leveraged her success at a time of segregation to generate social good. She refused to attend the ticker tape parade held for her honor in Tennessee because they planned to segregate the crowd. The banquet to celebrate her in Clarksville, Tennessee, was the first time that blacks and whites had gathered for the same event in the town's history.

Wilma overcame incredible odds and personal failures along the way through the support of community, family kindness, and personal grit. After her 1960 win at the Olympics, she retired from amateur athletics to finish college. She became a schoolteacher, athletics coach, and mother of four children.

Wilma Rudolph was inducted into the United States Olympic Hall of Fame and the National Track and Field Hall of Fame. She wrote an autobiography and there was even a movie made about her life. But her greatest accomplishment was creating the Wilma Rudolph Foundation, a not-for-profit community-based amateur sports program.

> **"The most important aspect is to be yourself and have confidence in yourself...the triumph can't be had without the struggle."**
> **—Wilma Rudolph**

Wilma Rudolph died of brain cancer at age fifty-four on November 12, 1994 in Nashville, Tennessee. Said Bill Mullican, a 1960 Olympic teammate, "She was beautiful. She was nice. And she was the best. That is something we can all aspire to."

Believe in yourself. Even when you feel like a failure, keep pushing. Give your very best not for fame, not for glory or success or dollars; those aren't the real rewards. Keep pushing because you can make a difference in other people's lives. That's what it means to matter.

> *"Life is not easy for any of us. But what of that?*
> *We must have perseverance and above all confidence*

in ourselves. We must believe that we are gifted for
something and that this thing must be attained."
Marie Curie, first woman to win a Nobel prize

COMMUNICATE BELONGING

"Communication leads to community, that is, to understanding, intimacy and mutual valuing."
Rollo May, psychologist

What do you do when you feel marginalized? When you feel excluded, sidelined, and the exception to the norm?

My daughter, Sarah, spent her last two years of high school attending community college classes. She received both her high school diploma and an Associates of Arts degree on her eighteenth birthday. She stepped up to the plate and swung for the fences! It is a rare accomplishment that required tremendous self-motivation, determination, and fortitude. But therein lies the difficulty. She was an exception to the norm.

Every time she called the high school to ask about

getting what she needed, she hit a wall. Unintention-ally, the very nice office ladies spoke to her in ways that left her feeling marginalized. They couldn't compre-hend her frustration when they informed her that she could pick up what she needed during lunch or plan-ning period. On a Tuesday. High school students go to school at the high school with the same schedule as all the other high schoolers; what is so confusing? Except Sarah attended classes at a college campus across town with a completely different schedule. I'm sure they meant well. Bless their hearts.

Not long ago, my husband and I went on a vacation road trip. We tried listening to an audio book, but I kept pausing it every few minutes to rant about the non-inclusive language used by the author. Repeatedly, the author referred to "mankind" and "all men" when what he really meant was all humanity. It is a legitimate pet peeve of mine. If you mean "all people," just say that. In trying to listen to the book, we had to wade through and mentally translate marginalizing language. If the author of the book and the office ladies at the high school had been more inclusive in their speech, more aware of their audience, meaningful communication could have transpired. Instead, the listeners became frustrated and disengaged.

It is your responsibility to communicate in a way that people want to listen and understand.

Imagine the above illustrations in a business setting. If you communicate in a way that marginalizes the one on the receiving end of your communication, most likely, you'll lose a customer and never know why. The customer will go somewhere they feel seen and heard, not marginalized.

Pay attention to how you communicate, whether spoken or in writing. Do you use inclusive, open, and welcoming language that invites further dialogue? Seek feedback from others to see if they understand what you intended to communicate. If they don't, ask clarifying questions, then modify and adapt. It's not just the right and decent thing to do, it is the savvy thing to do. In the professional world, your ability to communicate a sense of belonging will translate to dollars. When individuals feel they have been seen and heard, they will happily spend their money with you as a customer, a client, or a boss.

"You have a responsibility to make inclusion a daily thought, so we can get rid of the word 'inclusion.'"
Theodore Melfi, screenwriter

PERMIT YOURSELF AN OCCASIONAL
PITY PARTY

"Self-pity in its early stage is as snug as a feather mattress.
Only when it hardens does it become uncomfortable."
Maya Angelou, writer

*W*hen was the last time you felt sorry for yourself? Was it five months ago, five days ago, maybe five minutes ago? It is a natural human response, especially when things, seemingly not our fault, go wrong. I was hit by a semi-truck and spent 118 days hospitalized. That merits a good measure of self-pity.

For the first four years, my mental muscles labored determinedly to avoid feeling sorry for myself. Self-pity loomed like a black tar-pit hole at the edges of my mind. Imagine the Pit of Despair in the movie *Princess Bride* and you have a pretty good idea what I'm talking about. (If you haven't seen the movie, stop reading right now and go rent it. I'm embarrassed for you.) I was terrified that if I got too close, I would get sucked in and never come back. Under the circumstances, that made a lot of sense. So, I put on a smile and forged ahead like a champ. Everyone I knew praised my "positive attitude." I was amazing! Or so I was told. Stoicism in the face of overwhelming adversity garners great respect, even awe. My devastated sense of self badly needed the affirmation and unrelenting optimism. My imaginary Pollyanna companion carried me through the darkest days. She served a valuable purpose…until she didn't.

To never feel sorry for yourself denies the fullness of your humanity. Somewhere deep in the recesses of your brain, you know you are not being honest. Eventually your brain will rebel as you double down on repressing grief. It takes more and more effort to fight the voice of unhappiness that gets louder and louder. Believe me; I know.

The more you avoid something by pushing it away, the more energy you give to something you don't want, and the less energy you have for what you really do want.

What if it is perfectly fine to feel sorry for yourself? What if you give yourself permission to go to the pity party? Sometimes things just plain suck and it is okay to admit it. Go to the pity party with all the bells on. Shoot, wear a tiara! Just remember to only stay long enough for the appetizers; you have a curfew. Give yourself a time limit. That's what I do now when I feel sorry for myself, I'll just own it.

In 2018, I got a phone call after an ordinary dermatology exam. The nurse casually informed me of a basal cell carcinoma on my leg, one of the most common types of cancers in the world, easily removed with a mostly painless procedure. But the C-word! As a kidney transplant patient, I take immunosuppressive medications for life to prevent organ rejection. That puts me at vastly higher risk of skin cancer complications. I'm fine, but hearing the C-word made me mad.

I grumbled to God, "Oh, for crying out loud, have I not been through enough? I mean really!" Then came guilt. I'm alive, after all, and supposed to feel grateful. All. The. Time. After more than four years of relentless gratitude, I snapped. I mumbled to myself, "Why not feel sorry for myself for a little while? Not very long. I'll just go to the pity party, have appetizers, some chip and dip, then go home and call it good." So that's what I did. I wallowed for a little while, just long enough to enjoy that cozy feather bed feeling. Then I pulled myself back up and went on with living.

Don't ever feel guilty for being honest about your needs.

If you need to feel sorry for yourself a little bit, that is perfectly okay. Pour yourself a glass of wine (or a juice box), run a bubble bath, and settle in for a glam little pity party. Call a trusted friend. Say, "Hey, I need somebody to listen to me and feel sorry for myself for a little while. Will you just tell me that I'm okay and completely justified for like five minutes?" Once the water in the tub goes cold, time is up. No refilling with more hot water; that's cheating. Get up, pour a cup of coffee, and get on with living.

"In life, you can blame a lot of people and you can wallow in self-pity or you can pick yourself up and say, listen, I have to be responsible for myself."
Howard Schultz, former Starbucks CEO

FINANCIAL LITERACY MATTERS
SOONER THAN YOU THINK

"Why are people so tired on April first?
Because they just finished a 31-day March."
Unknown source, corny Dad joke no one will claim.

*N*ationally, April fifteenth is one of the biggest days of the year—TAX DAY. April is also National Financial Literacy month. My brother is a Certified Financial Planner and our dad is a retired financial advisor. Fortunately for me, old fashioned attitudes around money run in the family. You can watch a funny and informative video of my brother and me drinking cocktails—Old Fashioneds, of course —and talking about financial literacy. Did I forget to mention that April is also national alcohol month? Which makes sense after taxes.

As a young woman, I received a financial literacy education that I have tried to pass on to others.

Moments before landing in the catastrophic collision that forever changed my life, my two young employees and I were listening to the audio book *Rich Dad, Poor Dad* and discussing how they could save money for the future.

Your most valuable asset is *time*.

Investing your money in diversified mutual funds is really the simplest way to go. The best way is with a good financial advisor. Historically, looking at long-term outcomes and assuming average rates of return, money invested in the stock market doubles approximately every seven years. It's brilliantly known as "the rule of seven." Here's the key, you don't need a lot of money. You just need to start. Because money doubles on average every seven years, that means a twenty-year-old who waits to start investing until thirty-four years old, when they feel more established, has missed two doublings of their money. What kind of a difference do you think that makes? It can make the difference of millions of dollars. Millions?! Yes. Meet the power of compounding interest. Simply put, and not to insult your intelligence, compounding interest means earning interest on your interest over time.

To illustrate, would you rather have a million dollars right now or would you rather have a penny and double that amount every day for the next thirty days? A million dollars now? Or a penny today and double that amount tomorrow, then double that amount the next day, and so on for the next thirty days? Most people want the million dollars now. Let's check that out…

- Day One: You have a penny.
- Day Two: You have two pennies.
- Day Three: You have four pennies.
- Day Four: You have eight pennies.
- Day Five: You have sixteen pennies.
- Are you feeling rich?
- Day Six: Thirty-two cents
- Day Seven: Sixty-four cents
- Day Eight: One dollar and twenty-eight cents… and so on.

Now let's see what happens….

- Day Twenty: You have $5,242.88. Okay, that is pretty nice from starting with a penny, but it is nowhere near a million dollars.
- Day Twenty-four: You have $83,886.08, which is mighty impressive. But it is still not a million dollars.
- Day Twenty-six: You have $335,554.32.
- Day Twenty-seven: You have $671,088.64. By now you are getting the picture.
- Day Twenty-eight: You have $1,342,177.28. Now hold onto your hat….
- Day Twenty-nine: You have $2,684,354.56.
- And on Day Thirty, you have $5,368,709.12!

That is the power of compounding.

Let's go back to what I mentioned earlier about the difference between investing at age twenty and waiting until you're thirty-four to begin. Let's assume you invest $1,200 a year starting at age twenty. That is a whopping $100 a month. You could come up with that in coffee money. Let's assume an average annual rate of return of 10 percent from age twenty to age thirty-four on $1,200 saved per year. And then you stop; you never invest another dime. At age sixty-five, you will have invested a total of $16,800. That feels doable.

Now, if you start investing at age thirty-four and you invest $1,200 a year, every year for thirty-one years, until you're sixty-five years old, you will have invested a total of $37,200. Which scenario nets you more money at retirement age?

In the second scenario, where you invested more than thirty-seven thousand dollars over the course of thirty-one years, at retirement age, you will have $241,365.32. In the first scenario, in which you invested a total of $16,800 over fourteen years, but you did it from age twenty until age thirty-four, you will net at retirement $731,822.31. That is a difference of half of a million dollars!

You don't need to find numbers fascinating, but you do need a fundamental grasp of financial literacy.

Hopefully, you will get serious about saving money as soon as possible. So, what next? Do you tuck it under your mattress? What do you do? Find a principled financial advisor to help you invest in a solid diversified mutual fund. Don't watch the stock market on a daily basis because all that will do is freak you out. Instead, keep adding to your investments consistently and watch it compound over time.

"Compound interest is the eighth wonder of the world. She who understands it, earns it. She who doesn't, pays it. Compound interest is the most powerful force in the universe." That paraphrased quote has been attributed to Albert Einstein. Undoubtedly, he didn't exactly say that, but when asked to name the greatest invention in human history, Einstein did reply, "Compound interest."

"Money is only a tool. It will take you wherever you wish, but it will not replace you as the driver."
Ayn Rand, author

TAKE TIME FOR BALANCE AND REST

"One swallow does not make a summer, neither does one fine day. Similarly, one day or brief time of happiness does not make a person entirely happy."
Aristotle, philosopher

The highest goal of any human being is the pursuit of happiness, so says Aristotle and many other philosophers, including the founding fathers of the United States. My culminating paper for a degree in Philosophy analyzed *The Nicomachean Ethics*, one of Aristotle's best-known works on ethics. In it, he explained and justified the "morality of the mean"—in other words, the benefits of keeping to the middle, balanced. Extremes lead to unhappiness.

Sometimes, happiness demands that you chill out, calm down, be still, and maybe take a nap. Your body and mind need rest and gentleness. Things get out of whack from time to time. Highly driven people espe-cially need to plan for regular downtime.

Balance a staccato rhythm with a slower pace.

I used to quip, "I'm like a toddler. I have two speeds, full stop and full go." I went at full go for about fifty weeks of the year, and then I crashed. Other than a couple of weeks off in December, I lived pretty much at a pedal-to-the-metal pace. I missed out on a lot and made myself sick while pursuing perfection instead of happiness.

It's important to understand what takes energy from you. Weirdly, for example, writing emails costs me a lot of energy. I don't know why. What activities demand a lot of energy from you? How about people? Who takes extra energy? Sometimes we refer to those as E.G.R. people—Extra Grace Required. Every single one of us is only given the same twenty-four hours of every day, and every single one of us has a limited supply of energy. If you don't budget your time and energy wisely, it will drain you of happiness as you try to make everyone else happy.

Where you give your energy, you give your life.

Are you giving your life to the pursuit of happiness? That doesn't mean pursuing pure fun all the time. Not all things are fun. Happiness may come from the satis-faction of paying your bills. Having healthy teeth makes me happy; so, I floss even though that isn't exactly fun. And sometimes happiness is the joy of sitting outside on a beautiful summer evening, enjoying conversation and maybe a glass of wine with a friend. There is a season for everything. A time to work, a time to floss, and a time to rest.

Take time to create balance in your life. Live life in all its joyful gloriousness. You will be happy you did.

"We hold these truths to be self-evident: that all [wo]men are created equal; that they are endowed by their Creator with certain unalienable rights; that among these are life, liberty, and the pursuit of happiness."
Thomas Jefferson, The Declaration of Independence

BE AN ORGAN DONOR

"You gain strength, courage, and confidence by every experience in which you stop to look fear in the face. You are able to say to yourself, `I lived through this horror. I can take the next thing that comes along.' ... If you fail anywhere along the line, it will take away your confidence. You must make yourself succeed every time. You must do the thing you think you cannot do."
Eleanor Roosevelt, diplomat and former First Lady

arch 14 is World Kidney Day and the entire month is designated National Kidney Month.

If you had said this fact to me before 2014, I would have smiled and raised my eyebrows approvingly, but I wouldn't have given it much thought as I bustled through my tightly planned day. Life has a way of drastically altering perspective. I wouldn't be alive today without the extreme care that doctors have put into kidney research and transplantation.

Kidney disease is the ninth leading cause of death in the United States. More than twenty-six million Americans have chronic kidney disease (CKD), and most don't know it. Of the 123,000 Americans currently waiting for an organ transplant, 82 percent of them need a kidney. The average wait time is 3.6 years.

Every day, twelve people die waiting for a kidney, in America alone. Be part of the solution.

If I had died on March 1, 2014, when I was hit as a pedestrian by a semi-truck moving sixty-five miles per hour, my organs would have been donated to someone in need. I have always believed in the value of organ donation. Fortunately, though, I survived. Unfortunately, my kidney function didn't. Doctors kept saying that they *should* come back, but by the end of the year, we were talking about transplant eligibility. I was devastated and sick, with kidney function hovering around 12 percent. Because of additional surgeries, they didn't put me "on the list" until June 2015.

Through a tremendous blessing, we learned that my thirty-six-year-old baby brother was a perfect match. He courageously stepped up as a living donor. Then we found out Matt is a freak. Well, we knew that, but I mean anatomically. He is one of less than 1 percent of the population with multiple arteries connecting to each of his kidneys instead of the usual one. Combine that with my extensive scar tissue and we learned that we had a case no doctor wanted to touch…or so we thought.

Enter the University of Maryland Medical Center and Dr. Stephen Bartlett.

According to Dr. Bartlett, "Kidney transplants using live donors with multiple renal arteries, an otherwise harmless anatomical irregularity affecting small numbers of people, comprise only about a dozen of the many hundreds of total kidney transplants done at UMMC each year."

Make it a priority to put others before yourself.

Whether it means placing the needs of your team above your own, setting aside your personal desires for the greater good, or literally sacrificing a part of your body to save another, a genuine leader acts with courage.

I was honored to witness acts of courage from leaders at all levels during our dangerous kidney transplant. My brother showed leadership by offering himself as a living donor, a surgery that is almost, if not equal to, that of the receiver of the organ. The team at UMMC showed courage in trusting the leadership of Dr. Bartlett who exercised true valor in taking on a high-risk case.

Whether it is a wish you have for after death or if you want to take a step further and become a living donor, be brave and help save a life. Then make sure everyone knows and spread the word.

> *"Unless someone like you cares a whole awful lot,*
> *nothing is going to get better. It's not."*
> *Dr. Seuss (Theodor Seuss Geisel), author*

USE YOUR PAIN TO HELP OTHERS

"Dumped? Fired? Scorned? Humiliated? Totally pissed off? If so, I've got great news! You might be on your way to living your best life ever—if you consciously choose to channel this pain into fuel—and use it to motivate yourself to become your highest potential self!"
Karen Salmansohn, author

*M*any people believe that when something bad happens—especially something really bad—a deep cosmic motivation is at work. You hear, "Everything happens for a reason." And, "God has a plan!" The cognitive dissonance caused by bad things happening to good people puts our brains on tilt. We seek to justify traumatic events and how they will affect a now altered future.

Sometimes life hits you like a truck.

Don't let it make you a victim.

When you say everything happens for a reason, you get stuck waiting for the good, hoping it will come sometime in the future. What if instead of waiting for good to come, you choose to act now and create that good? Instead of allowing yourself to get lost in your own story of pain and heartache, seek opportunities to reach out to others; not in spite of your pain and disappointment, but because of it.

On a flight in 2017, one such opportunity took a seat next to me on the airplane in the form of a distressed young woman. After casually chatting briefly, our conversation turned personal and we both shared our stories. She was moving to Seattle while dealing with health problems serious enough that a kidney transplant might be necessary. I seized the chance to share my experience, talk her through the procedures, comically show off my medication collection, and offer what words of comfort I could. We parted ways with tears and hugs as she smiled and thanked me for calming her fears.

This young woman will never know that the seat next to me was originally reserved for a colleague who had to cancel at the last minute due to his own serious health problem. Funny how life works out.

Bad things will happen. Tragedies will occur. At times it's going to feel incredibly overwhelming. When that happens, try asking, "Who can I help?" Seek opportunities to create good in the world. Somewhere, there are people who need the empathy that you can uniquely provide. Respond proactively and positively instead of staying static.

The choice is yours to make. And who knows? Maybe that opportunity is sitting right next to you—not in spite of the bad things, but because of them.

"The best way to not feel hopeless is to get up and do something. Don't wait for good things to happen to you. If you go out and make some good things happen, you will fill the world with hope, you will fill yourself with hope."
Barack Obama, 44th president of the United States

YOU ARE WORTH IT

"You have a destiny, you are a human of intrinsic value,
you were born to fulfill a mission."
Sunday Adelaja, Ukrainian pastor

What is your life worth?

To the medical community, the price for my life was 2.5 million dollars. Because of ongoing healthcare, the cash register continues to ring regularly. Money isn't all that has been paid. The price for the life I'm blessed to live was a deeply costly sacrifice on many fronts. For example:

- Over $54,000 from 440 donors across North America to a GoFundMe campaign.
- Countless hours, days, weeks, and months spent by family members to care for me.

- An unspeakable number of casseroles generously delivered to our house.
- Fear, worry, grief, and bruised knees from hours of prayer by family, friends, and strangers.
- Traumatic memories that can never be erased from the minds of everyone involved in or connected to the wreck.
- Giving up our family's home, the only one our children have known, due to lack of wheelchair accessibility.
- Our lives forever affected by the countless minor changes that major trauma brings.

Many people have sacrificed greatly and paid a heavy price for my life, including me. I try to live worthy of such a steep price. Only then can I turn the enormous investment into value for others.

My problems aren't any worse than yours, only more dramatic. Maybe. A tremendous price has been paid for all our lives. None of us goes through life alone, even though, at times, it feels that way. When you consider all that you have received, perhaps as non-dramatic as encouragement from a friend, you realize our interconnectedness.

Gratitude shifts your perspective and lightens any burdens you are trying to carry on your own.

Make your own list. What have you and others sacrificed or given freely that enables you to contribute to the world? Who has helped you at every step? Who gave up time, money, or their own plans? What price have you paid to learn the lessons that inform your understanding now?

I've been asked many times, "Elisa, if you could go back and change things, would you?" Without hesitation, I answer, "No." It would be fabulous if it could hurt less; but I wouldn't change it. The lessons learned along the way, the contributions I can now make because of my experiences, are worth every indignity and agony. The price was steep, but worth it.

The world needs what only you can uniquely bring, and a price has been paid. No matter how steep the cost, your contribution to the world is worth it. Don't hold back. You are valuable beyond measure just for who you are.

"No matter how dysfunctional your background, how broke or broken you are, where you are today, or what anyone else says, YOU MATTER, and your life matters!"
Germany Kent, journalist and author

"LIVING 5 RULES"

1. It's not about YOU.

Be of service to others.

2. Actually CARE.

Practice genuine compassion.

3. ASK more, tell less.

Keep a curious and open mind.

4. DO the hard thing.

Give 100% of your presence, attention, & effort.

5. PLAY the long game.

Patiently invest in people with kindness.

* * *

For fifteen years, Elisa Hays, CSP, served as the Founder and Chief Daydreamer of an entertainment company that helped over 30,000 kids a year strengthen confidence in their creativity. As a creative designer and entrepreneur, she also holds patents-pending in the United States and Canada for the invention of a play-based hand washing system that makes cleaning hands fun and educational.

After surviving devastating trauma and selling her company in 2014, Elisa dedicated her life to helping others thrive amidst disabling circumstances. As a

Certified Speaking Professional—a designation held by less than 13 percent of professional speakers globally— she presents at conferences internationally and consults with businesses on empathy fueled leadership, resilience, and inclusion. As a Certified ADA Coordinator, she advises organizations on improving access to programs and services for people with disabilities.

Whenever possible, she visits with individuals coping with critical injuries and illnesses.

Elisa lives in Washington state with her family and codependent service dog named Belle.

For more information or speaking inquiries, please visit https://www.ElisaHays.com.

Made in the USA
Columbia, SC
05 February 2020